H★MILTON

AN AMERICAN MUSICAL BY LIN-MANUEL MIRANDA

CONTENTS

ISBN 978-1-70513-103-9

Visit Hal Leonard Online at
www.halleonard.com

Contact us:
Hal Leonard
7777 West Bluemound Road
Milwaukee, WI 53213
Email: info@halleonard.com

In Europe, contact:
Hal Leonard Europe Limited
42 Wigmore Street
Marylebone, London, W1U 2RN
Email: info@halleonardeurope.com

In Australia, contact:
Hal Leonard Australia Pty. Ltd.
4 Lentara Court
Cheltenham, Victoria, 3192 Australia
Email: info@halleonard.com.au

ALEXANDER HAMILTON

Words and Music by
LIN-MANUEL MIRANDA

Play 4 times

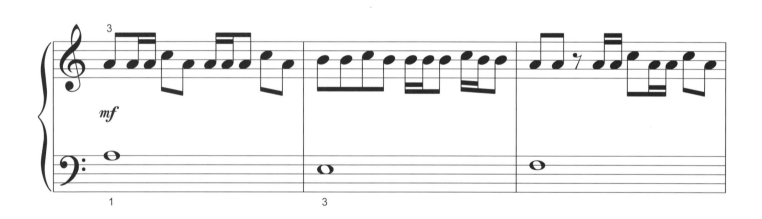

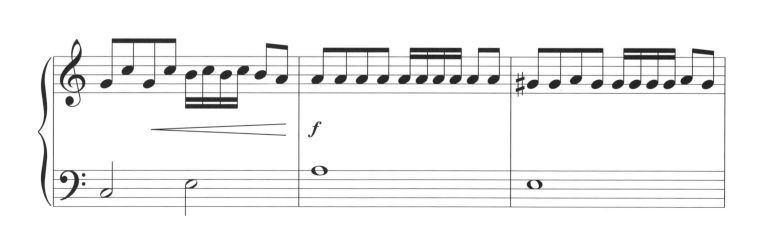

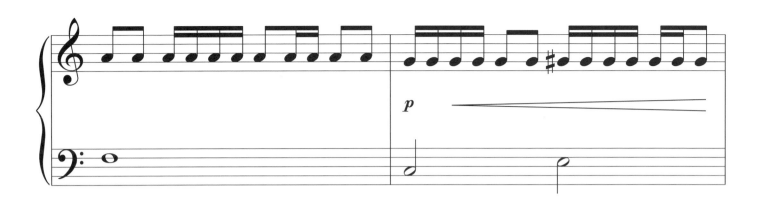

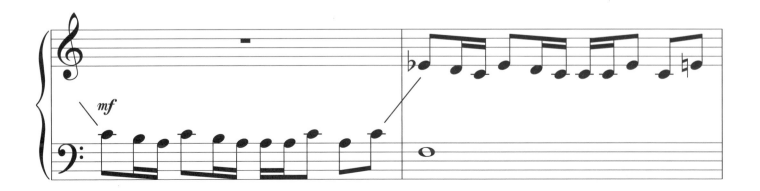

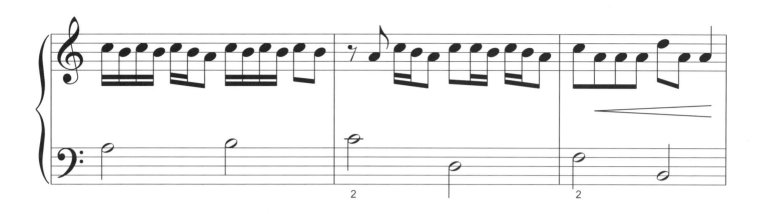

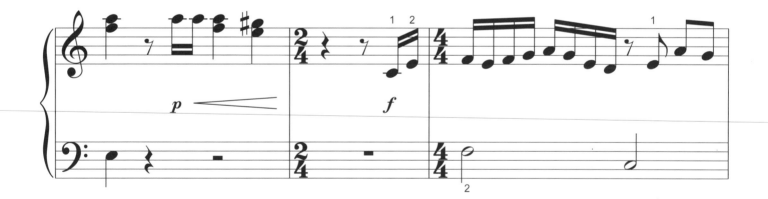

DEAR THEODOSIA

Words and Music by
LIN-MANUEL MIRANDA

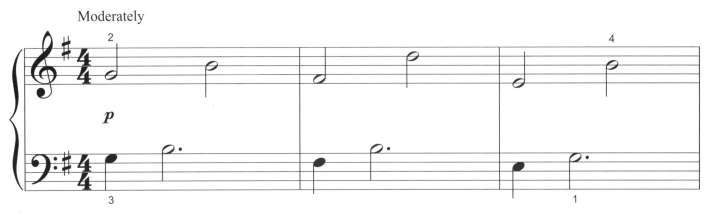

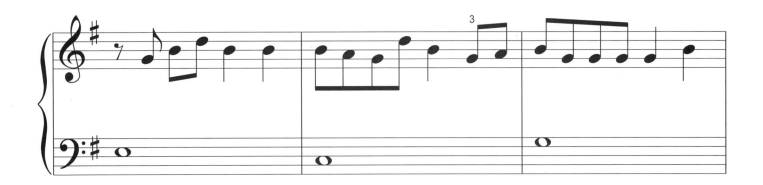

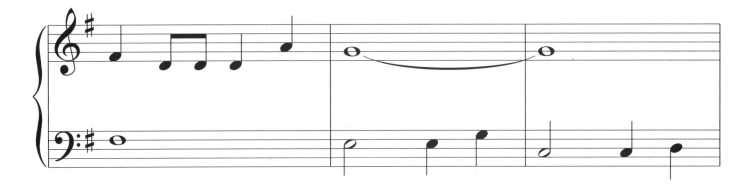

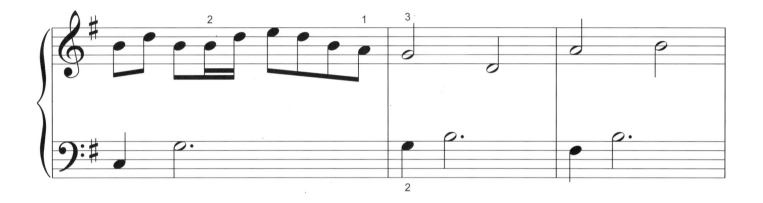

To Coda

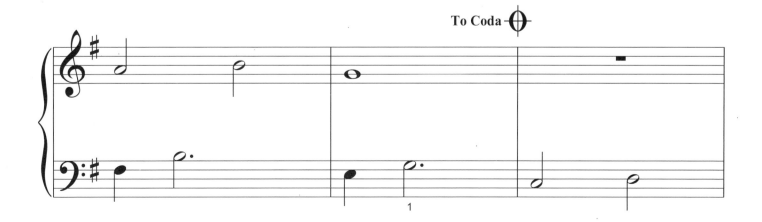

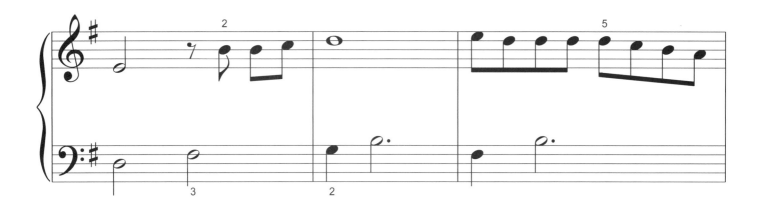

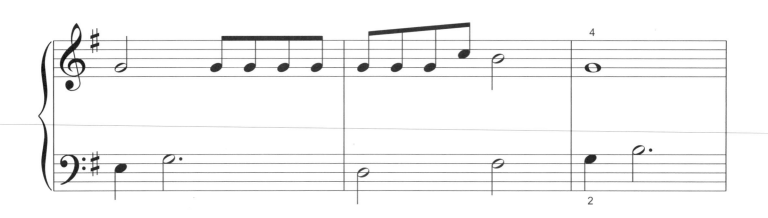

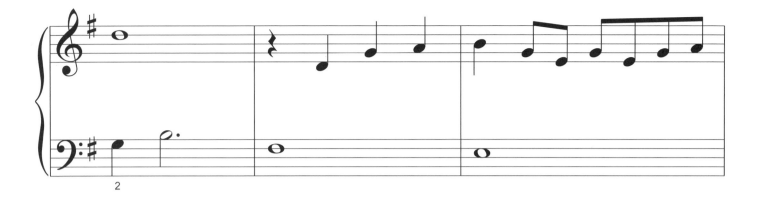

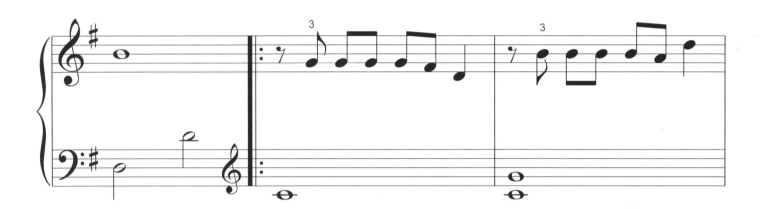

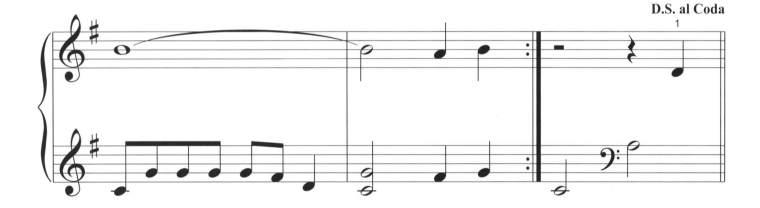

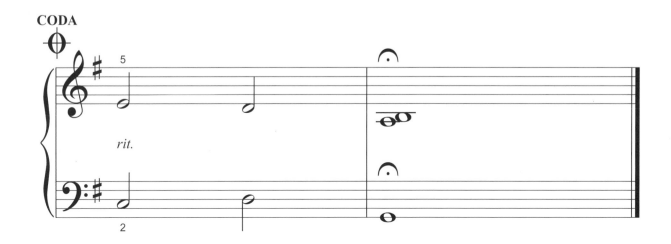

HELPLESS

Words and Music by
LIN-MANUEL MIRANDA

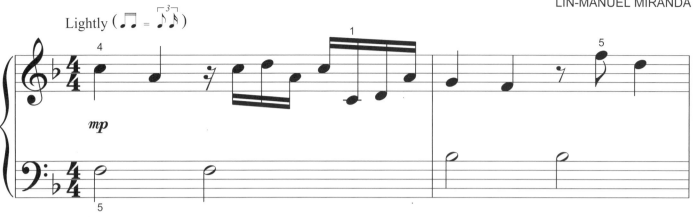

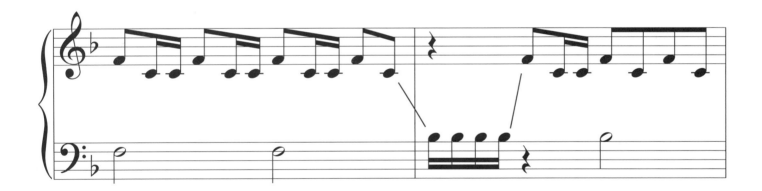

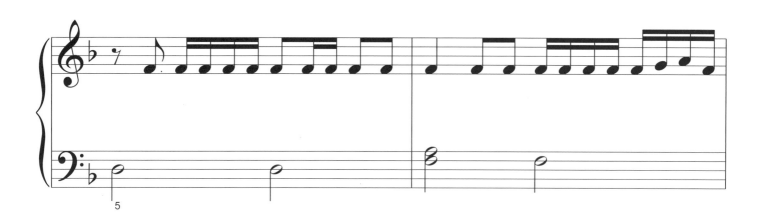

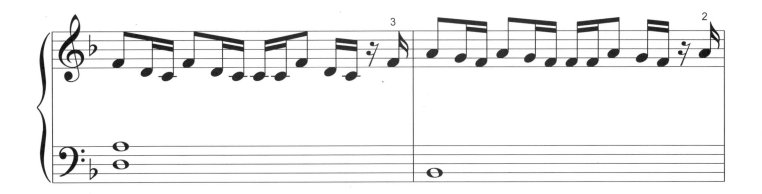

IT'S QUIET UPTOWN

Words and Music by
LIN-MANUEL MIRANDA

Slowly

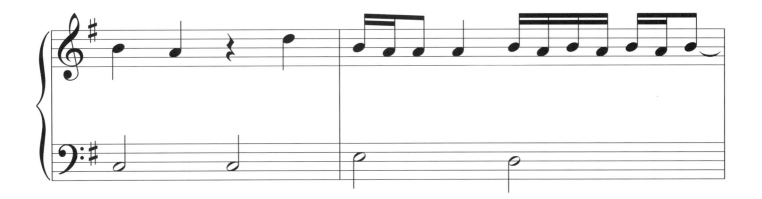

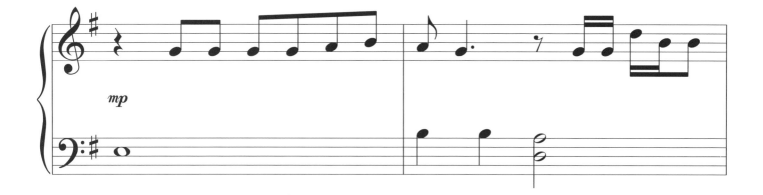

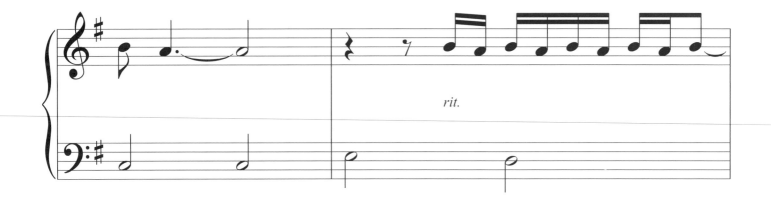

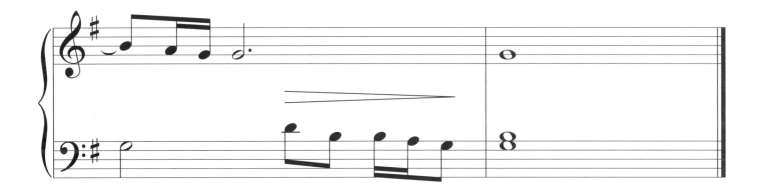

ONE LAST TIME

Words and Music by
LIN-MANUEL MIRANDA

Moderately

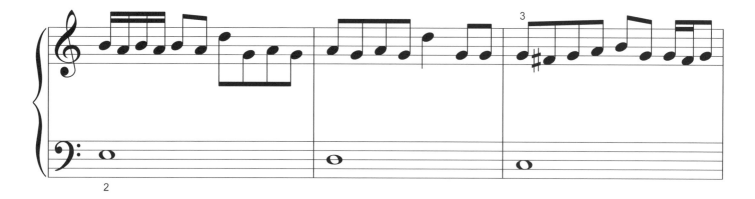

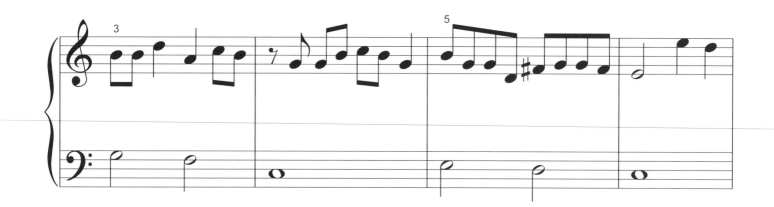

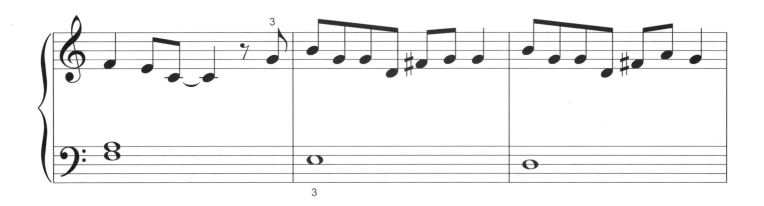

MY SHOT

Words and Music by
LIN-MANUEL MIRANDA
with Albert Johnson, Kejuan Waliek Muchita,
Osten Harvey, Jr., Roger Troutman, Christopher Wallace

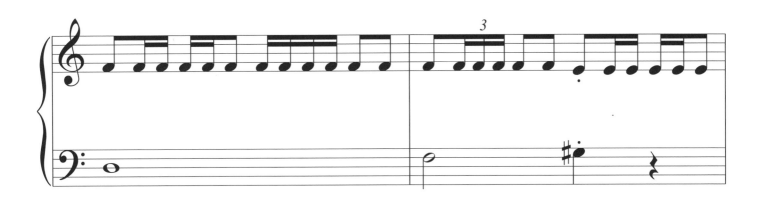

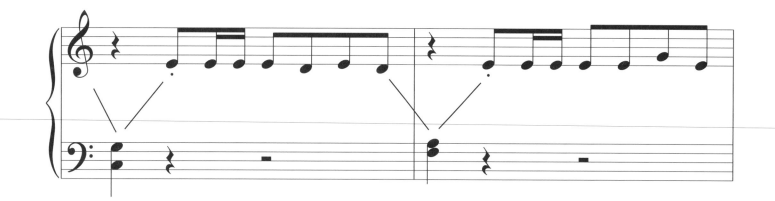

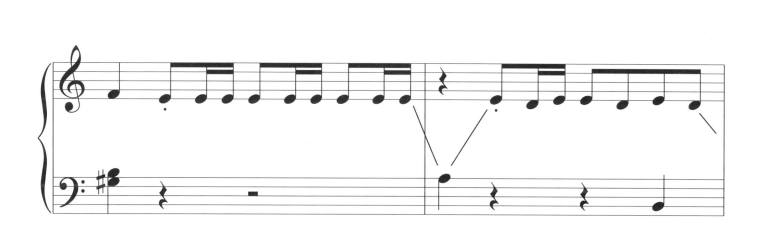

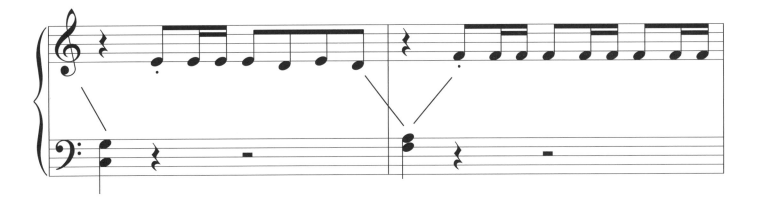

THE SCHUYLER SISTERS

Words and Music by
LIN-MANUEL MIRANDA

Moderately, rhythmic

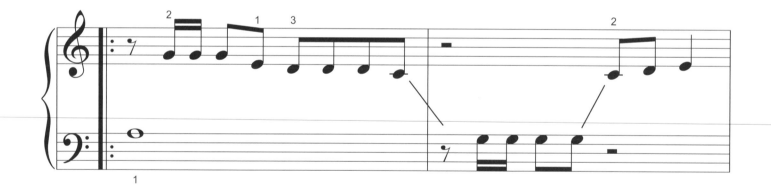

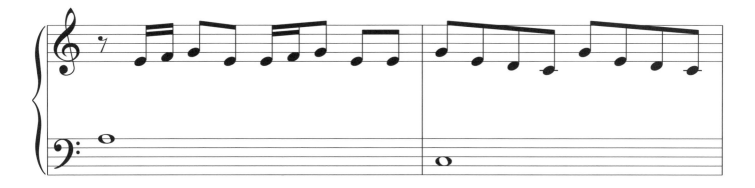

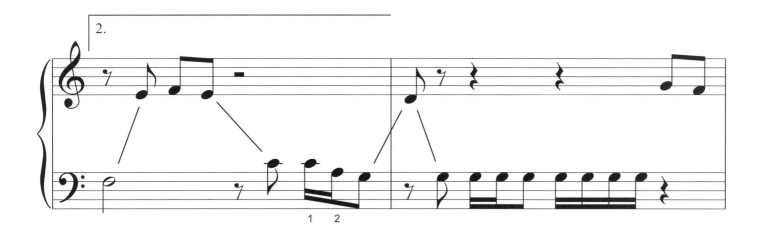

1   2

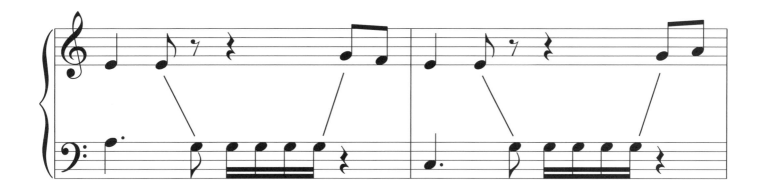

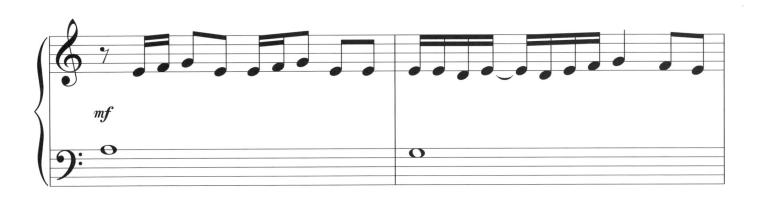

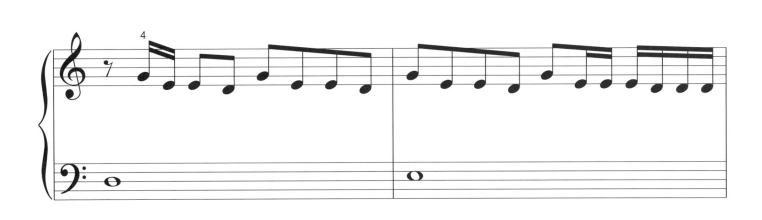

34

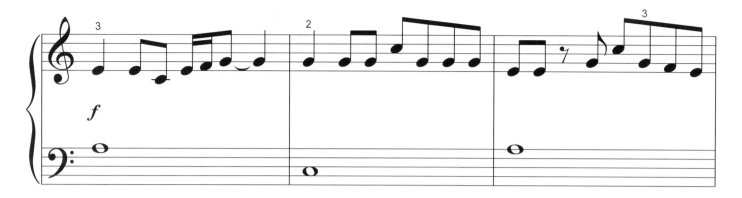

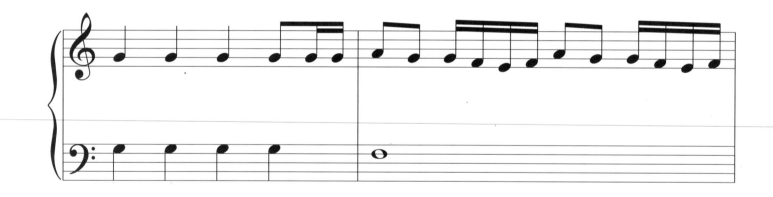

WHO LIVES, WHO DIES, WHO TELLS YOUR STORY

Words and Music by
LIN-MANUEL MIRANDA

Moderately, in 2

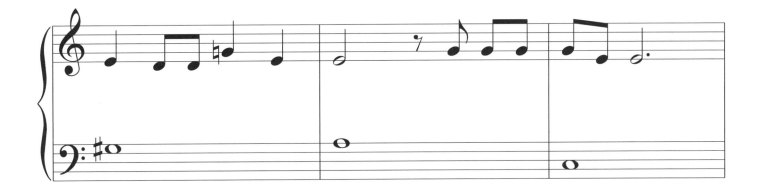

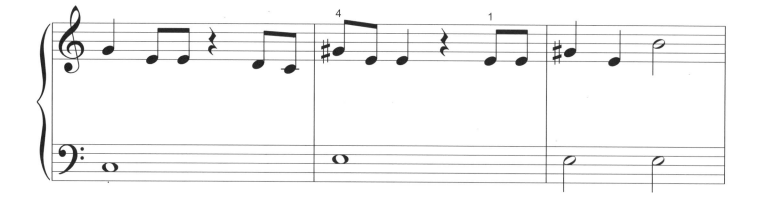

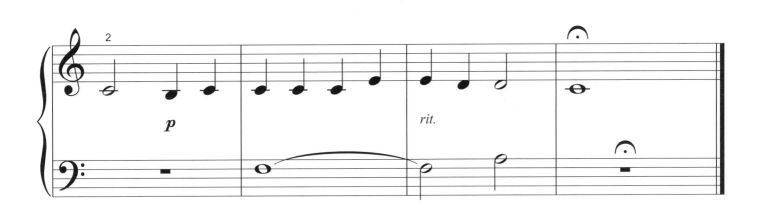

THAT WOULD BE ENOUGH

Words and Music by
LIN-MANUEL MIRANDA

Slowly

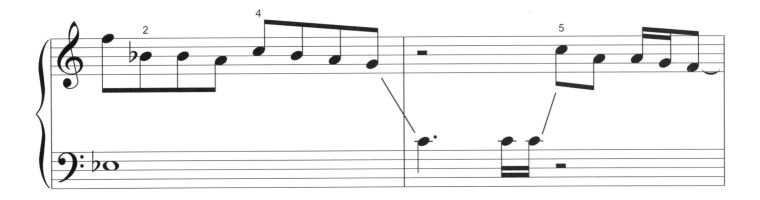

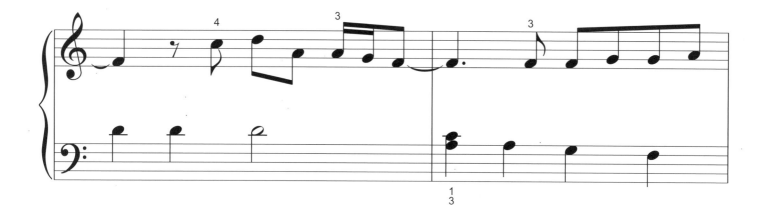

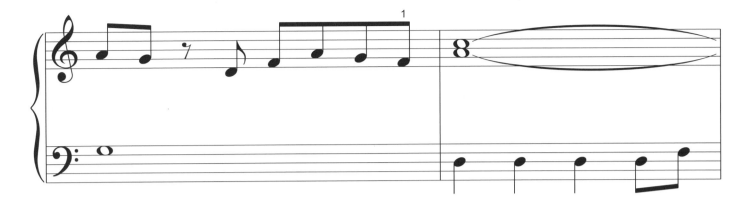

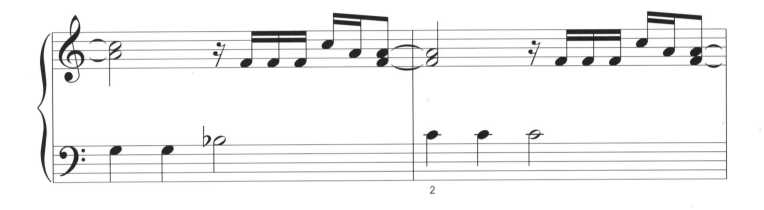

YOU'LL BE BACK

Words and Music by
LIN-MANUEL MIRANDA

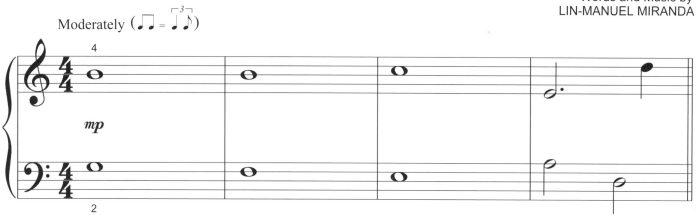

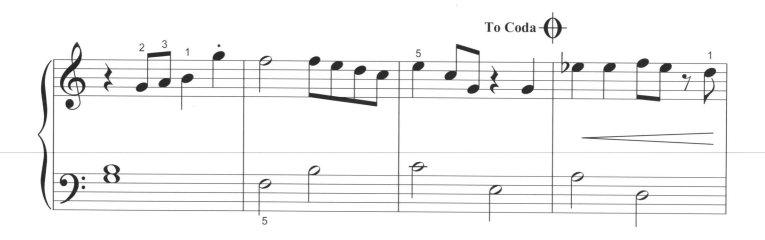

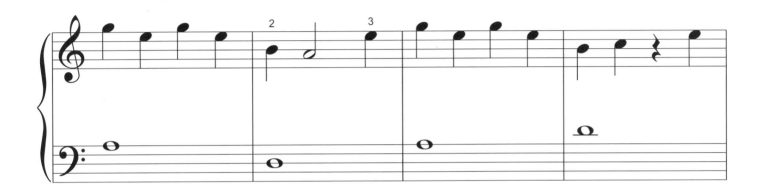

D.S. al Coda

CODA

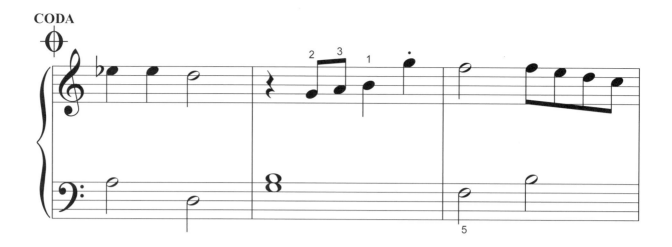

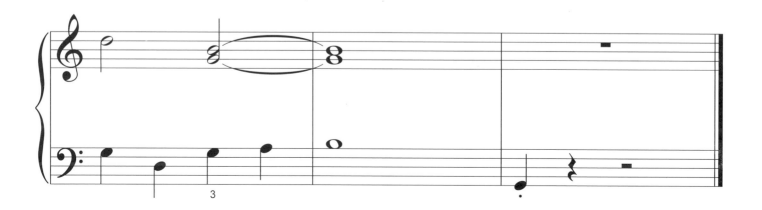